The Ultimate
Multiple Mini Interview (MMI)

"Confidence comes from being prepared."

If you ordered this eBook you probably have an MMI interview in the near future. Don't stress. I was in the same exact position you were in, and unfortunately, I could only work with the limited amount of resources available to me online. MMI interviews are a relatively new interviewing strategy medical schools and other healthcare graduate programs are implementing to assess prospective candidates. After researching online, reading books, gathering information from medical school friends, and most importantly, **attending 7 multiple mini interviews myself**, I sought to create this eBook to demystify the MMI process for you.

I will begin by explaining what the MMI is all about and later outline the **PRINCIPLES** that you should learn. The MMI is all about these principles. What I mean by this is if you can learn the main principle, **you will be able to confidently respond to the scenario despite the extra fluff or varying details they provide.** This is how you do well at the MMI.

For every principle I have also generated **key buzzwords** that you should mention during your response. These buzzwords are what drive the response home and is what instigates the interviewer to think, "This person knows what he/she is talking about."

Lastly, have fun with the MMI! You will soon find out that is more like a gameshow than an interview. **The process is much more enjoyable when you know how to attack each station.**

By Hayk Hakobyan, MD Candidate
Georgetown School of Medicine
UCLA BS

Disclaimer: The scenarios mentioned in this eBook were written by me and are NOT from the interviews I have attended.

TABLE OF CONTENTS

General Points

Outline of Multiple Mini Interview (MMI)

Outline of Multiple Mini Interview (MMI)

- -

"Priming your brain into thinking you have encountered this situation will relieve any unexpected nerves during the actual day."

I want to begin by describing the general process of the MMI. Based off of my experience, the MMI process usually has 8-10 stations. You will have approximately two minutes to read the prompt located outside of each station and anywhere from 5-8 minutes to respond (depending on the interviewing school).

If there are 8-10 stations that means there are 8-10 applicants just like you. You are each given 8-10 stickers with your name on it. Each time you enter a new station, you will give this sticker to the interviewer in that room. They use this sticker to keep track of who answered what in each station.

Majority of stations will be a scenario prompt that you will respond to. Depending on the school, you may also have an acting/role-playing station, a teamwork station, or a typing station. I have encountered all of these types, so it is better to be prepared for them than assume you may not encounter it.

Before I did my first MMI, I had several accessory questions in my head. "Should I shake the interviewer's hand? Should I wait to be seated? Should I knock before I enter? How should I start my response? What if I forget the details in the scenario?" **I will clarify all of these questions for you now.**

Outline of Multiple Mini Interview (MMI)

Here is a general overview of EXACTLY what happens at a typical station:

- Buzzer goes off to read prompt outside of the door. It may be a buzzer or someone on the speaker phone that announces, "You may start reading the prompt."
- You read the prompt for approximately two minutes. You may be given paper and a pencil to write notes. If you really **understand the principle** behind the scenario you will not need anything but yourself.
- As you read, pay close attention to "who" you are in the situation. Are you a physician? A friend? This will give you a better idea of what role you are given and what you need to do in the scenario.
- **Stay calm and be confident.**
- Buzzer goes off to enter the room. **You do not need to knock**. There are 8-10 other people interviewing before or after you. Imagine if everyone had to knock? The interviewer is already expecting you. Just go ahead and enter.
- **Your vibe will carry the tone as soon as you enter the room.** This is really important. If you are shy and nervous, this will resonate through the room. Keep in mind that you only have 5-8 minutes with this interviewer. You want to be **energetic, positive, and confident**. This balance of enthusiasm and being poised will set the tone for the rest of that station. You want to start off on this note.
- Enter the room, smile and say hello! The interviewer will **either be sitting down or will stand up to greet you.** I have had both happen to me. Despite this, I always tried to give them a firm handshake. Regardless, you will need to give them the sticker with your name on it, so you might as well get a handshake out of this transaction.
- After giving them a sticker, go ahead and sit down. Do not wait to be seated. You will look vulnerable and there will be an automatic shift in power between you and the interviewer. Remember, the interviewer is just another human being and you are interviewing the school as much as the school is interviewing you. Keep that in mind.

Outline of Multiple Mini Interview (MMI)

- As you sit down, the interviewer will always ask you, "Did you get a chance to read the prompt, if so, what did you think of it?"
- This is where you respond to the prompt.
- After your response, the interviewer will have anywhere from 2-4 rebuttal questions. You will respond to the rebuttal questions. Keep in mind that the interviewers are trained to be stoic during your responses. **Don't use their facial expressions or body language as a metric to measure your performance during your response. Stay confident all the way through.**
- If they are done with their rebuttal questions and there is time left, they may ask you if you have any questions for them.
  - If the interviewer is a faculty member, I usually take this time to ask a question about the school or their thoughts on a certain aspect of the curriculum, school related topic, or their position. **Remember to keep this conversational.**
  - If the interviewer is a medical student, I will ask them about their experience at the school. **Remember to keep this conversational.**
- After 5-8 minutes, the buzzer will go off for you to leave the room.
- Stand up, shake the interviewer's hand again, and say, **"It was a pleasure meeting you. Have an amazing day!"**
- Leave the room and rotate to the next station. Don't have any lingering thoughts about the previous station, and get yourself pumped for the next station.

You should read this twice and imagine yourself in a typical scenario. Priming your brain into thinking that you have encountered this situation will hopefully relieve any unexpected nerves on the actual day.

Despite understanding how typical scenario works, I still have not elaborated the most important part of this whole process. **How should you respond to the scenario?**

RESPONSE TIPS

Scenario Response

Scenario Response

"Priming your brain into thinking you have encountered this situation will relieve any unexpected nerves during the actual day."

This by far the most crucial aspect of the MMI. I like to think that responding to a scenario is an art. I say this because everyone will be responding differently and will approach the situation at different angles. In the past, I have heard that there is not a single right answer, but there are many wrong answers. I disagree with this partially and would like to rephrase this.

There is a common RIGHT approach to every scenario and there are many WRONG approaches you can take. Most applicants fall in between this. They will respond correctly and address the whole scenario to a few stations while missing the point for others. **Your goal is to respond appropriately to all but one station that may be off the wall.** Some medical schools will drop your lowest score on a station, so you want the "off the wall" scenario to be that one.

Have you ever wondered why medical schools are implementing the MMI? It is because with traditional interviews you can prepare answers and give them a scripted, disingenuous response. The MMI is a whole different beast. You will need to think on the spot and come up with an answer within two minutes. **The idea is that your response is a reflection of what you really believe and think 99% of the time.** It is much more of an effective tool to evaluate your readiness for the multi-faceted situations in medicine and if your **mentality** is up to par with being a healthcare professional.

Although this may be true and an effective method to evaluate applicants, I sincerely believe this misses a crucial point. **You have probably never encountered such scenarios in your life.** You may be the most genuine person and the most mature individual out of your friends, however, you may have a hard time responding to scenarios if you have not encountered it. This will result in a poor evaluation on your part – which is exactly why it is imperative that you **understand the principles** in the following sections.

Scenario Response

Here is WHAT the MMI is evaluating on and HOW you should respond to the different scenarios. Keep in mind this is the same concept for all the scenarios.

- **MMI is testing you on how open-minded you are.** With that being said, DO NOT fall into any extremes. If a situation requires you to assess two sides to a story, you will need to **paint the picture** for the interviewer. Meaning, you will have to explain both sides and point out the pros and cons of each side. **This shows that you understand the full scope of the scenario.** When giving your actual answer, it will merely be "leaning" towards that direction but you "understand why someone would disagree because of reasons A and B." Imagine if you enter a room and immediately pick one side of the scenario to defend - AVOID this at all costs. This is a complete trap and it will definitely mess you up when the interview hits back with rebuttal questions. On the other hand, if you paint a whole picture for the interviewer, **you will probably address some of the rebuttal questions in your answer.** This is what you want.

- **MMI is testing you on how effectively you can communicate.** Imagine you enter a station and start rambling on the topic without any discrete organization of your words and response. The interviewer will likely assume you do not have a good grasp on the concept and will probably give you a poor evaluation on your communication. This is why you need to **speak with conviction. The most effective response will be delivered in the first two minutes.** You want to get to the meat of your response.

- **MMI will challenge you to defend or discuss your personal opinions.** This kind of ties to the first point, but you need to avoid strong language. Remove "always, absolutely, never" in your vocabulary. It is likely you are not being empathetic to the full scope of the scenario if you use this language in your response. Furthermore, there are moments you can integrate your personal experiences into your response. I did not do this for every scenario (as it may not be applicable), but when I was able to I found it was an effective method to keep the exchange memorable. You can also apply general working knowledge to issues that are relevant; however, I would be cautious of doing this. Avoid bringing up opinions on politics or other topics and issues you are not well informed on. You will likely fall short and sound like you do not know what you are talking about.

Scenario Response

If you want to stay updated on ethical issues you can find more information at this link below. You probably will not need to if you understand the principles behind each scenario, but it is a great reference.

http://depts.washington.edu/bioethx/topics/index.html

INTRO TO PRINCIPLES

MMI Principles

MMI Principles

"Knowing these principles will allow you to confidently respond to any scenario."

As I mentioned before, understanding these principles is the key to responding efficiently and correctly to each station. It really does not matter whether you are dealing with an 11-year-old boy as a patient or a Jehovah's Witness, **as long as you understand the principle you can apply it to any scenario.** This is how you do well on the MMI. **You recognize the principle behind each scenario, and retrieve the important steps that will lead you to the correct approach.**

Here are the most common principles you should know for the MMI:

• Respecting Patient Autonomy

• Being Ethical Requires Honesty

• Cultural Competency

• Self-Reflecting For An Unbiased Approach to Resolve Issues

• Miscellaneous Reasoning

These are the most common principles that I have encountered during the MMI. Of course, there will be stations you encounter that may not directly fall within these principles; however, **knowing these principles will allow you to respond confidently to any scenario. I repeat, knowing these principles will provide you the knowledge and proper frame of thinking required to approach any scenario.** You will instantly recognize the lingo and the can use the correct approach in any scenario.

Along with an explanation of each principle, I have provided multiple scenarios and an ideal response to each. Carefully review my responses. It will give you the stepping stone and the correct frame of thinking to fully understand the concept from each principle.

CHAPTER 1

Principle: Respecting Patient Autonomy

Principle: Respecting Patient Autonomy

"Balance between respecting patient autonomy and acting in the best interest of the patient."

I am listing this principle first because I constantly saw this scenario come up in every MMI that I went to. After actually answering multiple versions of this scenario you will recognize there is a common approach to this kind.

The idea behind these kinds of scenarios is **that the patient has wishes that will go against your traditional line of thinking and rational**. Very simple. The patient will either refuse treatment/medication, request unorthodox treatment styles (Chinese medicine, Eastern medicine, herbal, etc.), or will have any other request that is outside of what you may think they should be doing.

You are usually a physician or a healthcare professional in this scenario. Here is the basic outline for your response:
You **educate yourself** on the matter by collecting information on the topic (if applicable), present this to the patient in an **unbiased fashion**, give the patient time to come to a **uniform decision** about their health, and **offer care** regardless of what path they take. **It is a fine balance of respecting patient autonomy and acting in the best interest of the patient.**

A common variation to this situation is when the patient or person of interest is physically or mentally incapable of making the decision on their own. During this situation, you need to assess if they are **competent enough** to understand their situation. If they are physically or mentally incapable to make that decision, you will need find more information to serve in their best interest while respecting their wishes. This will make more sense after reading the scenarios below.

Buzzwords:
- Respect patient autonomy
- I will educate myself first
- Present information in an unbiased fashion
- I will make sure patient is competent to understand their situation
- Fine balance between respecting patient autonomy and acting in their best interest
- I will follow up regardless of what decision they make and continue to offer care

Principle: Respecting Patient Autonomy

---

1. Refusing Vaccination

You are a physician and a mother with her 5-year old daughter comes into your clinic. The mother seems adamant about refusing to get her child vaccinated. She genuinely believes that vaccinations are correlated with autism and does not want to take that risk. However, it is known that a lot of diseases have risen because people don't get vaccines. Discuss what you would do.

This is an interesting scenario because I took a course that was related to public health and we talked about the correlation between vaccines, autism and other disabilities. This situation shows the complexities of respecting patient autonomy and also trying to act in the best interest of the patient. As any great physician, you also have a role to be an educator. Especially in a situation like this, education plays a major role. I would first do research on the scientific evidence behind the correlation of vaccines and autism or other proposed disabilities/illnesses. By doing research I will gather concrete information from viable sources and research articles. My goal would be to present this information to the patient's mother in the hopes of being as objective as possible. I would also discuss the public perception of vaccines and how accurate these perceptions are based on the research I have done. I would guide the patient and her family throughout this process; however, I would give them the platform to make an informed decision at the end. Hopefully, with my help and guidance, they will make the best decision for their child. Whatever decision the patient does make, I would follow through with them and monitor their health, and give them that branch for them to reach out in case they do need further care.

Rebuttal Question: Will you be persuasive when you give her the information you researched on?

I think persuasive is the wrong term to use in this scenario. I won't be persuasive, but rather informative as possible. My hope would be to give them the full scope behind vaccinations and autism so they can make a confident and decision.

Principle: Respecting Patient Autonomy

Rebuttal Question: Let's say you 100% know vaccinations does not cause autism. How will you allow the patient to refuse their 5-year old child vaccinations?

I know, it is a complex and tough scenario to be in. As a physician and an educator, I need to do my part in providing information so that the patient can make his/her own uniformed decision based on all the facts for their health. With that being said, I understand that I will encounter situations where a patient's decision may go against the traditional line of belief and understanding. It is important to remain professional and give them that platform for them to decide. Which, again, despite which decision they do make, I will regularly follow up and offer them care.

Notice how the interviewer will try to press you on your stance. It is important to stay confident during these rebuttal questions. Knowing the main principle, you should feel calm and recognize that the interviewer is just trying to test your opinion. Also, take the time to really understand your line of action here: educate yourself, educate the patient, and offer help regardless of decision. There may be rebuttal questions regarding what you are educating yourself on, or how you will present information to the patient, etc. You will be able to answer those with ease.

2. Belief System Goes Against Treatment

You are a physician at a local hospital and you encounter a Native American child who needs to get a liver transplant. It is imperative that the child remains at the hospital for the next available liver transplant. The family requests to get discharged to go back to their home to practice an important ritual that is common for children his age. As soon as he wants to get discharged, there is an available liver for transplant and is ready. Discuss what you would do in this situation.

This scenario depicts the complexity of respecting patient autonomy and acting in the best interest of the patient. In a situation like this, and as the role of a physician, I would want to guide the patient to make the best-informed decision. I would sit down with the patient and their family and discuss the realities of the difficulty of availability and finding another donor that is compatible, the risk that they may not receive another liver from someone, and essentially what is at stake in case they do leave for the ritual.

Principle: Respecting Patient Autonomy

Although I would want to act in the best interest of the patient, I would also respect their wishes. I would provide them with the all this information, and give them the platform to decide. I would not mandate what I think is right over their belief system. I would also follow through with the patient, even if they leave for the ritual. I would give them that branch and follow up with them if they continued to seek care.

The same line of action applies here. It does not matter if traditional line of thinking is challenged because of religious beliefs, practices, or traditions. You need to respect patient autonomy.

3. Birth Control Pills

You are a doctor and a 14-year old child comes in with her mother. She requests that her mother sit outside as you see her in one of the patient rooms. As you ask her regular follow up questions, she asks you for birth control pills. She begs you not to tell her mother because she is embarrassed. What would you do?

This scenario depicts a real and complex situation. Do we give a minor birth control pills without parental consent? To actually come to this decision, I would ask the child follow up questions after her request. For example, I would ask her if she is sexually active, what they know about safe sex, and what they know about the birth control pill. I would also inform her that managing pregnancy will not remove the possibility for sexually transmitted diseases. My hopes would be to find out why she does not want her mother to know. By asking her these questions, my goal would be to educate her on the matter and have her fully understand the consequences of her decision. As a physician, I would respect patient autonomy while looking out for her best interest. After providing her with such information, I would see if prescribing birth control pills to minors without parental consent is legal. If it is, I would give her time to think about this decision, and if she still wants the pills after being informed, I would prescribe it. Despite giving her the pills, I would make sure she is happy with the care she received and will give her that platform and comfort to reach out in case she had any more questions or concerns.

Principle: Respecting Patient Autonomy

This scenario is a little more difficult because of the added twist of the patient being a minor. Regardless, you should notice that respecting patient autonomy applies to **everyone**. You should also notice that you may not be explicitly educating the patient but rather guiding them to a healthy decision. This is especially important when the patient is incompetent or too young to understand.

4. Cancer Patient Refusing Traditional Treatment

You are an oncologist and you just did a test on a patient to assess if he has cancer. After finding out that the patient does in fact have cancer, you start going over treatment options and present this to the patient. With traditional treatment, the patient will have 5 years to live. Without treatment, the patient will only have 1 year to live. Despite providing treatment options, the patient wants to pursue alternative medicine. Discuss your approach in this scenario.

This scenario shows the complexity of respecting patient autonomy and our duty as a physician to act in the best interest of the patient. In order to better assess their decision, I would ask what kind of alternative medicine the patient is pursuing and their scope of knowledge behind this specific approach. After doing so, I will educate myself on this treatment option. During my research, I would find scientific based evidence to see whether this treatment option is a viable approach to eradicate the cancer. By doing so, I can present the information I found to the patient in an unbiased fashion. I will also mention that the standard treatment can prolong their life and make sure they understand the consequences of their decision. My hope would be to give them time to come to a uniform and final decision on this matter. Despite whichever decision they do make, I will be the best physician I can be to help them throughout this process.

5. Down Syndrome

You are an OBGYN physician and a patient who is 18 years old comes into your clinic. This patient is pregnant and has down syndrome. The parents are with her and are encouraging her to have an abortion because it may be a burden to raise this child. The patient wants to keep the baby. What would you do in this situation?

Principle: Respecting Patient Autonomy

This is a difficult situation because we need to address multiple issues. I would begin by asking the patients multiple questions to assess if she fully understands the realities of being pregnant and raising a child. Some of these questions would be what she knows about pregnancy and about being a mother and caring for a child. I would also ask the parents what the learning level of the child is and find out more about their concern for their daughter. My goal would be to assess if the patient is competent to understand her decision. After careful evaluation, if I recognized that the patient realizes the magnitude of her situation, I would respect her decision to have the baby. On the other hand, if she is mentally and physically not capable of taking her of the baby, I would try to seek help from psychological supportive services or other health counselors to help the patient come to terms with the option of an abortion. Whichever path this situation takes, I would offer the best quality of care and make sure the patient receives the help she needs.

6. Unconscious Patient

You are an ER physician at a local hospital. As you clock in for your shift, you approach your first patient in one of the patient rooms. The patient is an 18 year old girl and is unconscious on the hospital bed. The nurse rushes over to you and explains she desperately needs a blood transfusion. You realize that if she does not receive this blood transfusion, she will ultimately die. As soon as you begin the protocol for the blood transfusion, the nurse finds a Jehovah's Witness card in her pocket. You know Jehovah's Witnesses are 100% against blood transfusions – they will rather die than receive treatment. If you are unable to make a decision, this card will make the decision for you. Discuss what you would do.

This is such a difficult situation to be in. This is especially tough because the patient is unconscious and their life is on the line. My natural intuition would be to save this person's life, but I would first need to find out more information on the patient before coming to a decision. For example, I would try to see when this card was signed, if she was competent during the time she signed the card, and if she understood the implication of refusing treatment. To help me answer these questions I would hope I have the time to contact her family.

Principle: Respecting Patient Autonomy

Despite trying to act in the best interest of the patient, I would respect the patient's wishes if her family confirms and the answers I gathered reflected that she indeed did not want treatment. Respecting patient autonomy is important, despite these difficult scenarios where the patient may lose their life.

Notice that you must go great lengths to find out what the patient's wishes are even when they cannot physically tell you. Again, hone down this concept and you will be able to apply it to any scenario.

CHAPTER 2

Principle: Being Ethical Requires Honesty

Principle: Being Ethical Requires Honesty

"...describe the actual difficulty of being honest in these tough situations."

This principle is fairly straightforward and as the title implies, honesty is key. You will be put in a position where you will need to be ethical and honest. This is really important because as a healthcare professional, there will be moments where you will encounter mistakes in caring for a patient. With that being said, you want to sound as genuine as possible when you respond. Of course the right answer is to be honest, and most applicants will respond by stating the obvious answer in this scenario (even if it means saying you would inform a professor their best friend cheated in their class. This is probably something you wouldn't do). **Do you think this comes off as genuine to the interviewer? Probably not.** Instead, your response should describe the difficulty of being honest in a particular situation.

There is a huge difference between:

A. Yes, I will tell on my best friend because cheating is unethical and unfair to everyone else in the class.

B. It would be really tough to tell on my best friend. I would not want to hurt everything he/she has worked for in his/her academic career. With that being said, I would talk to him/her and try to come up with a solution for this predicament. If we could not reach a conclusion, I would be forced to tell the professor.

Again, most students will answer like point A. It is a common route to take when you have never encountered this scenario and only have two minutes to come up with a response. The key here is to **show the interviewer that you are being genuine by describing the actual difficulty of being honest in these tough situations.** This will definitely come off as being **honest** to the interviewer.

Principle: Being Ethical Requires Honesty

----

1. Accidental Dose

You are a medical student doing a clinical rotation on the surgical floor at a community hospital. It is early in the morning and after rounding, the surgical team members have departed for the operating room. You are about to go into a room to speak with the patient about her diabetes medication. The attending nurse pulls you aside and informs you she gave the patient 5 times the regular ordered dose of her blood pressure medication 20 minutes ago. The nurse has tried to page the surgery team twice but has been unsuccessful. You are the first person to be notified of this new information and the nurse tells you that the patient is currently stable and comfortable. Will you tell the patient about the accidental dosage? Discuss course of action you would take and explore the issues pertinent to this scenario.

I'm the first to be notified by the patient's nurse that a medical error was made resulting in her receiving 5 times the prescribed dose of her blood pressure medication. Even though the patient is currently stable and comfortable, the most pressing issue remains patient safety. She should be carefully monitored for any changes in discomfort or symptoms. I would next address this medical error with full disclosure to my supervisor, the surgical team and to the patient. By telling the patient that a mistake has been made, this would probably affect her outlook on the quality of care she has received. However, only by being fully honest and accountable do we stand the best chance of regaining her trust. To better understand why a mistake has been made, I would want to speak in more detail with her nurse regarding the exact surrounding circumstances in the hopes that similar errors could be prevented in the future.

I want to emphasize that **every** applicant will say they need to tell the patient the truth. So how can you make your response different? You really need to go into detail with what is at stake in telling the patient the truth. This takes deeper understanding and reflection on the matter. Notice that I explicitly describe the shortcomings of telling the patient in such a scenario to show the interviewer the difficulty of being honest.

Principle: Being Ethical Requires Honesty

2. Cheating Friend

If you are in class with a close friend, and they ask you to cheat off you or you notice them cheating during a test. How would you approach the situation?

This is a tough and realistic situation that can happen to any student. As a close friend, I would hate to put him/her in a situation where they would potentially fail the class or be expelled from school. On the other hand, it is also unfair and unjust to the rest of the students if he/she continued to cheat on the test. Considering both of these sides, I would confront my close friend after the exam and ask them about their actions. By doing so, I would hope to give them a comfortable platform for them to discuss any concerns or problems they may have been going through that led to them cheating on the test. Although there shouldn't be any excuse to justify him/her cheating, I would offer my guidance and help as any close friend would. I would also explain the realities and consequences of him/her cheating and that I would be forced to be in a position to notify higher school authorities if it continued. If he/she continued to cheat even after confronting him/her about their actions and resolving any issues, I would be forced to make that tough decision to notify the school administration.

Notice there is a healthy balance of being a good friend and being ethical in such a situation.

3. Disclosing Missed Results

You are a family physician with a busy clinic. Your next patient, Mr. Smith, is an elderly gentleman who has been under your care for his type II diabetes, asthma and recurring angina. He was last seen by you 5 weeks ago. You quickly review his chart prior to seeing him and to your disappointment you realize that his last electrocardiogram tracing done 6 weeks ago shows an abnormal ST segment elevation. The report was received in your office before Mr. Smith's last visit but you have not seen these results until now. Discuss what you would say to Mr. Smith with the interviewer.

Principle: Being Ethical Requires Honesty

I would begin by asking Mr. Smith how he is doing and if there have been any changes since we last met. Assuming no changes have taken place since our last encounter, I would start a conversation regarding the missed EKG result. I would notify him that he had an EKG test done 6 weeks ago and the results were placed shortly thereafter, but I did not see them until today. After acknowledging and being honest about my mistake, I'll let him know that I am in the process of setting up changes on how patient results are processed in the office in order to prevent this from happening again to anyone. I'll offer any support he needs regarding my mistake. When we are both satisfied with the discussion, I would shift gears and focus on Mr. Smith's current medical condition.

Usually with a medical error, you want to include in your response how you can prevent similar mistakes in the future. Doing so will make your response much stronger.

4. Shoplifting

You are shopping at a local grocery store. You notice a young male individual walk up to the aisle and take a product. They swiftly walk out of the grocery store and no one seems to notice. What do you do in such a situation?

First of all, I would be alarmed if something like this happened. I am not sure how my first reaction would be. If he swiftly walked out the door I would assume this individual was an employee of the grocery store, but then again, if he was not dressed in the employee attire that would be very skeptical. Without much knowledge, I would not want to jump to any conclusions, but as a shopper, I would go ahead and notify a nearby employee about what I just saw. My hope would be that they would go ahead and check the cameras in the grocery store and get to the bottom of this situation.

Principle: Being Ethical Requires Honesty

- -

Rebuttal Question: How will your viewpoint change if this was an older lady instead of a young male?

My viewpoint would not change entirely. It would be wrong to discriminate a younger male versus an older lady and assume that the male indeed had wrong intentions. In such a situation, I would treat the situation with an older lady the same way I would the younger male.

I included this rebuttal question because I want to show how two principles can be included in one station. Without being **culturally competent**, you may have treated the older lady differently than the young male.

CHAPTER 3

Principle: Cultural Competency

Principle: Cultural Competency

"Being an excellent physician has everything to do with being culturally competent."

I can almost guarantee that you will be asked about this principle in various forms. The biggest point I want to make about this is make sure to **be open minded and treat everyone with equal respect.** There may be scenarios that involve gay marriage, sexual orientation, sexual preference, and other culturally competent scenarios. You may be wondering why this is important as a healthcare professional. In order to explain, I included the definition of cultural competency in the healthcare setting:

Cultural competency – The ability to interact effectively with people of different cultures and socio-economic backgrounds without bias. Providers can deliver care that is respectful of and responsive to the health beliefs, practices, and cultural and linguistic needs of diverse patients. Developing cultural competency is critical to reducing health disparities and improving access to high quality health care that is respectful of and responsive to the needs of diverse patients.

Being an excellent physician or a healthcare provider has everything to do with being culturally competent. These scenarios will evaluate your thought process behind this concept.

Principle: Cultural Competency

1. Same Sex Parents

You are a senior medical student interested in becoming a pediatrician. It is the first day of your outpatient pediatrics elective. The staff pediatrician has asked you to tag along to see Matt, a 6-year-old child brought in by his parents with a cough. Shortly after the encounter, the staff pediatrician tells you they feel sorry for Matt because he has two dads. They believe that this is morally unacceptable because it will put Matt at increased risk for psychiatric disorders such as depression when he gets older. Discuss the course of action you would take in such a situation.

I would ask to speak with my staff in private, seek clarification and supporting evidence behind their comments. My main goal from our discussion is to improve the quality of care provided to Matt and future patients like Matt by not subjecting them to provider bias. However, by speaking with my staff this may negatively affect my chances of becoming a pediatrician. I am not sure how the staff pediatrician would view me after confronting him/her, but it would be morally wrong not to do so. I was in a similar situation at work where I interacted with my superior about management concerns and despite thinking that it was going to be job suicide, it ended up improving the dynamics of our work environment.

This scenario is mixture of honesty, ethics, and cultural competency.

2. Transgender

An individual who was born a male is looking to undergo a sexual transition. She has started taking hormonal therapy to begin her transition. Lately, she has been feeling abdominal pain and needs surgery unrelated to her sexual transition. You are a general surgeon that will perform the abdominal surgery on her. Before the surgery, she talks to you in private and asks you to keep her gender private. Meaning, you will have to all of the pre-surgery preparations yourself so your surgical team is unaware of her gender. Discuss your thoughts on this situation.

Principle: Cultural Competency

The idea of cultural competency comes to mind when I read this scenario. In such a situation, I would want to respect patient autonomy while acting in the best interest of the patient. This is obviously a very sensitive topic for the patient and as any physician would, it is important to be very empathetic in this situation. With that being said, I would sit down with the patient and discuss what I can do that is in my power to maintain her privacy throughout the procedure while also making sure the patient is safe. I would make sure she feels comfortable and at ease going into surgery. My goal would be to reach a mutual consensus where the patient feels comfortable with their privacy concerns and I feel comfortable that they are receiving high quality care.

Rebuttal Question: Let's say the patient is asking you to change the medical history chart from male to female so no one finds out about this. Would you do that for her?

I would discuss the legal implications of her wishes. For example, if I am legally allowed to switch the gender option from male to female on the patient chart than I would have no problem doing so. On the other hand, if this a legal issue, I would discuss alternative options for her to feel comfortable about her patient chart. With her permission, I would contact a health psychologist or a counselor that specializes in sexual transitions to help my patient any way they can.

Notice the interviewer can really press your opinion on a matter. Do not crack during this situation. If you went with the right approach, you should defend your answer.

CHAPTER 4

Principle: Self-Reflecting For An Unbiased Approach to Resolve Issues

Principle: Self-Reflecting for an Unbiased Approach to Resolve Issues

"By self-reflecting, you rule out any potential biases and address any that you may have first and foremost."

This scenario may come up during your MMI and if it does, I want you to be prepared. We have all been in a group project where that one person fails to the same amount of work. Resolving this issue may seem logical, but there is a big buzzword that will surely make your response more effective.

Self-reflection – The active and conscious process of placing emphasis and thought into one's character, actions and motives.

By self-reflecting, you rule out any potential biases and address any that you may have first and foremost. This is crucial in this particular scenario. You want to remove any judgment and biases you may have from the person of interest and strictly view the scenario based off of their performance. Secondly, I want to emphasize that disagreements inevitably arise among group work; however, to remain a cohesive unit, **any potential concerns should first be brought up to the remaining group members minus the individual(s) whom concerns have been identified.** Do not directly confront the member of interest without speaking to your other group members. **You want to remain a functional unit rather than an overly confident and aggressive team member.** After speaking with your group and establishing a group consensus, you may identify how to bring up the issues with the individual of concern. In the discussion make sure to address your concerns, group's concern, and any personal concerns raised by the individual of concern. This is also a great opportunity to **share your personal experience with the interviewer.**

Principle: Self-Reflecting for an Unbiased Approach to Resolve Issues

---

1. Group Member Not Cooperating

You are in a research team and have worked hard to publish a paper. One of the members in the group is the biostatistics expert and was enthusiastic about this project, but as soon as it is time to do work he is unreachable. Discuss the course of action you would take.

I would first take a step back and ask myself If I might have any personal bias towards this group member that could be contributing to my feelings of frustration. Afterwards, I would meet with my group without this individual present and see if other members had any concerns about this individual before sharing mine. Assuming we are all on the same page, I would offer suggestions on how to proceed and ask for group feedback. I was involved in a similar group work situation in my undergrad history course and we were able to move forward by exploring the potential reasons why our team member was unprepared and late for our sessions. Once I knew the reasons, I was able to offer support to help them. Having been through a similar experience, I wouldn't want to confront this individual on my own without first undergoing self-reflection and making sure I had the support of my group. My goal would be to see the root cause of the problem and try to communicate as much as I can to resolve the issue.

Rebuttal Question: What if this group member asks you to put their name on the publication?

After offering my support and giving this person the platform to express their concerns and problems, I would hope we can come to a mutual agreement to proceed further with the paper. If we do maintain mutual respect, we will continue with the group efforts to publish this paper and have this person's name on the paper.

Principle: Self-Reflecting for an Unbiased Approach to Resolve Issues

---

Rebuttal Question: Let us imagine that this group member fails to show up after offering your help. What would you do then?

I would look to see if the other group members can help with his portion of the work, and we would collectively find a solution that would benefit all of us. This may include that one of us has to learn biostatistics and do it ourselves or outsourcing this portion of the paper to someone else.

2. Group Member Not Cooperating Part 2

Each week you gather with your tutorial group to review material assigned to each team member from the previous week. The work is divided up among your group equally such that each team member is responsible for learning a specific aspect of the material and then reporting back to the rest of the group. You consistently feel frustrated with one member of the group who repeatedly comes to the group sessions late and unprepared. Discuss what you would do in this situation and be prepared to justify your response.

This is a scenario where I am a member of a weekly tutorial group and one of my classmates repeatedly comes to the sessions late and unprepared. I would first take a step back and ask myself if I might have any personal bias towards this group member that could be contributing to my feelings of frustration. Afterwards, I would meet with my group without the individual present and see if other members had any concerns about this individual before sharing mine. After reaching a mutual consensus with my group members, I would then approach the individual of interest. When doing so, I would make sure to be as empathetic and supportive as possible. We do not know what this individual may be going through, so it is important to not assume. Hopefully our discussion would be fruitful and we can get to the bottom of the root cause and issue.

Principle: Self-Reflecting for an Unbiased Approach to Resolve Issues

---

Rebuttal Question: Let's say this person avoids your phone calls and you cannot reach him/her. A week goes by and you see this person at school but as you approach him you smell alcohol from their breath. How would you respond?

It would be a very unfortunate to recognize alcohol being mixed in this situation, but I would not jump to conclusions. We do not know what this person is going through. I would do everything in my rightful power to help this person and be comforting as possible. At this point, it would be less about the group tutorial sessions and more about the health of this individual.

CHAPTER 5

Principle: Miscellaneous Reasoning

Principle: Miscellaneous Reasoning

"The key is to address all courses of action that you would take."

These are by far the hardest scenarios to get by. I mentioned this principle last because it will be a mixture of all the principles combined and more. You may bring in buzzwords from the previous principles and apply the frame of thinking you have learned in order to approach these reasoning scenarios. The only way you can really prepare for these kinds of scenarios is by practicing similar scenarios and getting used to the approach. **It will involve you thinking outside of the box.** It will test your rationalization skills and force you to come up with different solutions on the spot. Here are some pointers for you to focus on:

- **Paint the picture -** In my experience, I realized these scenarios are difficult because of their rebuttal questions. It is easy to take a one-sided stance on a topic, and have the interviewer directly counter your opinion with a rebuttal question. Bouncing back from this moment is hard. Again, do not fall in the trap of being one-sided. This will surely make you fall short and teach you that your original answer is counterintuitive. **Knowing this, you should address all sides to the story and <u>paint</u> the picture for the interviewer as much as you can so you don't fall short during a rebuttal.**

- **Collect More Information** - Your response in these scenarios will more or less require collecting more information from the person(s) involved in the scenario. You are not actually asking the interviewer for more details, but you will be merely exploring the different avenues of a response by how your patient/person of interest responds. **The key is to address all courses of action that you would take.** You will see examples of this in the scenarios below.

- **Combine Principles –** When articulating your response, keep in mind the principles you have learned. Remember that you must respect patient autonomy, be culturally competent, self-reflect, and be genuine in your response. You will soon see how these principles interplay with each other to give an effective response.

Principle: Miscellaneous Reasoning

1. New Drug

You are a head physician at the emergency room at a local hospital. There is a shortage of physicians, so the remaining physicians are working long hours in order to make ends meet at the ER. It has become increasingly difficult to stay awake and this may hinder the quality of care patients receive. The physicians start taking a new drug that helps their focus and concentration to endure these hours. Discuss what you think of this.

When considering such a complex situation, it is important to look at the whole picture. As these physicians take a new drug to stay awake, this may improve their concentration and compensate for the shortage of physicians in the short term, but this may have drastic effects in the long run. Considering this drug is legal or over the counter drug that can be bought, as the head physician, I would educate myself on this drug to understand its effects and possible dangers of taking such a drug. Even though this drug is legal, there may be drastic side effects that can cause harm in the long term. I would then present my findings to the rest of the physicians in the hopes of them coming to a uniform decision about their safety and health. I understand that even drinking coffee is a drug, but there are longitudinal studies that have been conducted on caffeine use to assess its dangers. With a new drug, one may not know its harmful effects until it is too late. I would also implement alternative methods to alleviate the exhaustion for working long hours, such as having mandatory breaks or naps during their shifts. Another option would be to promote physicians from other departments or hospitals to take on a few shifts at my department to alleviate some of the stress until we can find a more long-term solution.

Notice how my answer addressed rebuttal questions such as:

- We take drugs every day to stay awake. Why is it negative to take a new drug for staying awake?
- What other solutions can you think of to resolve this issue?

Principle: Miscellaneous Reasoning

By painting the whole picture for the interviewer, I was able to take into account these questions **before** they even asked it. This is the stance you want to take. It will show you know what you are talking about and that you are being open-minded to all facets of the scenario.

2. Hand Sanitizer

You are a doctor at the local hospital. A man comes in and goes up to hand sanitizer dispenser where he starts consuming it in large amounts. As a result, you notice the dispensers are often empty. What do you do?

In this situation, it is important not to jump to conclusions. I would approach this man in order to find out more about the situation. For example, I would try to find out if this man is an alcoholic, if he suffers from mental illnesses, and if he is an actual patient from the hospital. By understanding the background of this man, I would approach him in a cordial way. My goal would be to educate the man on the dangers of consuming hand sanitizer and how it affects hospital patients and staff. Afterwards, I would offer to get him addiction help and possibly contact him or his family to ask if this plan of action is okay.

3. The Gym

You just bought a condominium, and you get an added benefit which is the building's gym. There is a sign on the gym door that says residents only. You have a longtime friend from high school and she is looking to lose weight for the summer. She asks you to borrow your key to the gym. Explain your course of action.

Being in this situation is tough because I want to be a good friend and allow her to utilize the building's gym. Despite this, it would be wrong to the other residents if I disobey the policy of the condominium. I would first approach my friend and ask if she understands the policy for the residents only gym use. If she does understand, and it is due to financial reasons, I will help her find cheap gym prices around town. I would also evaluate her fitness goals and offer alternatives such as home workout videos or other exercises that can be done outdoors. Depending on her needs, I would devise a plan that would help her achieve her goals and abide by the condominium gym policy.

Principle: Miscellaneous Reasoning

4. Long Wait Times

The current average outpatient wait time in your area for an MRI scan is 120 days. This extended waiting period has sparked a growing concern from the general public who deems this wait time to be unacceptable. You are hired as a consultant to examine the current situation and to make recommendations. Discuss the course of action you would take.

This is a scenario where the public has grown concerned about the lengthy wait times to obtain an outpatient MRI scan. I recognize that this is a complex situation and after carefully exploring the issues of resource allocation and lack of resources, my recommendations would be to implement a provider tracking system to better understand how MRI appointments are being filled by physicians and to make changes to the way the MRI machines are currently being operated. In helping me arrive at my recommendations, I will research the factors that contribute to lengthy wait times. This may be inappropriate MRI machine operating hours or MRI scans being ordered for inpatients when they weren't indicated which may have further contributed to the lengthened the wait times for outpatient MRI scans.

5. Withholding Diagnosis from Minor

You are an oncologist and are taking care of a patient who is a 12-year old boy. Recently, you did a series of tests and discovered the presence of cancer cells in the child's brain. You realize your patient only has a few years left to live. As you prepare to discuss the results with the boy and his family, the parents stop you outside of the patient's room and ask you not to tell the boy the bad news. When you see the boy, he asks you what his prognosis is. Describe the course of action you would take in such a situation.

Principle: Miscellaneous Reasoning

In order to approach this situation, I would need to collect more information in order to assess the child's mental capacity to handle information about their prognosis. By doing so, I can fully understand the wishes of both parties in order to make a wise decision. For example, I would ask the patient questions about their illness and specific questions about the disease to gain his perspective and assess his maturity. My ultimate goal would be to understand if he will enjoy the remaining time of his life. If the patient shows signs of maturity to handle the situation, I would have a healthy discussion with the parents so we can all introduce this newfound information to the patient. On the other hand, if the child seems to not have the mental capacity to handle this news, I would be forced to respect the parent's wishes to withhold such information.

6. Selling Needles

You are a pharmacist at a local pharmacy. A patient walks in and requests needles and syringes. As you ask for their prescription, they explain that they do not have a prescription and need the needles and syringes for their health. You then check his records and find that the patient is not receiving any treatment for diabetes. Describe the course of action you would take. Specifically, would you sell the needles to the patient or not?

As a pharmacist and a healthcare professional, it is important not to jump to conclusions about this patient's need and use for needles. Despite the patient's demands, I would have to abide by the pharmacy's policy on syringe sales. However, I understand that the patient does not have a prescription, so it is important to collect more information to assess his intentions for buying needles. I would ask about his health and make him feel comfortable to talk about any problems or health concerns he may have. By doing so, I can have an open discussion in the hopes of the patient communicating their intentions for using needles. If we reach a conclusion that the patient needs the needles for a health concern, I would take the necessary steps to offer that care and consult about their health. On the other hand, if it is a drug-related need for needles, I would suggest needle exchange programs which allow drug users to exchange dirty needles for new ones for free.

Principle: Miscellaneous Reasoning

7. Limited Vaccine

There is an outbreak of an incredibly life-threatening disease. The disease is spreading across the country at a rapid rate and the survival rate is less than 50%. You are a senior health care administrator, and when the vaccine is developed, you have priority to receive the drug. Do you take the vaccine to yourself or give it to another person? Why or why not?

This is a real tough situation to be in. I think I can take two paths with this scenario. Initially, I would want to take the vaccine myself and give it to my family in order to make sure they are safe. However, when considering the whole country I must consider a practical approach. My decision will be based on how I can save the most people. As a health care administrator, I may have the knowledge and information necessary to save the most people. It really comes down to who is the most eligible to save more lives. If I am in that position I would take the vaccine and hopefully prolong my life in order to save more people. If the most eligible person ends up being someone else then the better qualified individual should take the vaccine.

Rebuttal Question: Let's say you are one of the first people to know about this life-threatening fatal disease and you are told by higher authorities to not share this information with anyone. Would you tell your family?

To be in a position to know about this disease first would entail a lot of responsibility on my part. To be honest, it would be really difficult to go home, see my family knowing their life may be threatened in any way and withhold such information from them. I would try my best to look at this situation and see if other people would be harmed by knowing such information. With that being said, and I am being totally honest, it would be really tough to stare into the eyes of my family members and suppress such information from them.

Principle: Miscellaneous Reasoning

- -

This is such a tough situation to be in. Notice how honest my response is. **Most applicants will not answer like this.** I can almost guarantee you that every applicant will say they will not tell anyone about the disease. Can you imagine the interviewer's reaction when you say this response? **It will be both refreshing and come off as more genuine to the interviewer if you are honest.**

8. Not Reporting Child Abuse

As a physiotherapist, you are referred a 16-year-old for treatment of severe burns that limit function on the patients arms and hands. Upon examination, you notice other burn marks and unexplained bruises on the patient. After working with the patient for a few weeks, you ask about the other marks on the patient's body. The patient admits to being abused by their parents but begs you no to tell anyone. What do you do?

If my patient admitted about his physical abuse, I would be as comforting as possible. I understand there is a psychological impact behind such a traumatic event, which is why the patient requested to not have his parents find out. In this situation, I would try to collect more information from my patient. For instance, I would find out how long the abuse has been occurring, what the motivation is for the abuse, and what the patient knows about child services. I would educate the patient about child services and provide information for them to feel supportive and know there are people available to help him. If my patient continues to be fearful and is adamant about not seeking help, I would consult with a more experienced person on the matter. Despite the hesitation and path we take, it will ultimately end up with the patient receiving care and help.

9. Patient Wait Times

In order to answer for the overflow in patient wait times and the decrease in time each patient has with the physician, some healthcare providers have suggested that patients with multiple symptoms or illnesses should see different physicians for each symptom. For example, a depressed patient that also has a cough should only be able to ask about their cough to a primary care physician while asking about their depression to a psychiatrist. Discuss what you think of this.

Principle: Miscellaneous Reasoning

When considering this suggestion from the surface, it would make sense for a patient to see a different physician for each separate symptom or illness. Taking this route may alleviate some of the patient wait times, however, this thinking misses a major point and I believe the quality of care being received will be hindered. A lot of symptoms are correlated with each other, which is why we have patient medical history charts and consider the patient as a whole when treating. In this specific scenario, the patient with the bad cough may have slowly gotten depressed because the cough has hindered their social interactions. I believe to be a good physician, you must consider all of the patient's health concerns and take the best course of action. Furthermore, this may alleviate patient wait times at certain clinics, but it will put a massive burden on the patient to see a different physician for every symptom.

CHAPTER 6

Teamwork Station

Teamwork Station

This scenario is interesting because you will have to team up with either another interviewer or two other applicants. I will explain both options so you may get a better idea.

- **Another Interviewer** – Let's say station number 6 is the teamwork station and you just finished station number 5. The prompt outside of station 6 will ask you to give instructions to another interviewer in the room. To clarify, there will be one interviewer that is watching/evaluating, and another interviewer with whom you will be teaming up with. As you finish station 6, you will proceed to station 7.

- **Two Other Applicants** – Again let's say station number 6 is the teamwork station and you just finished station number 5. The prompt outside of station 6 will ask you to give instructions to **another applicant** in the room. This means, you are the one giving instructions and there is another applicant receiving the instruction. As you finish station 6, the applicant you teamed up with will cycle to station 7 but you will not cycle to the next station. Instead, you will wait outside of station 6 again to re-enter, **but this time you will be the one receiving instructions and the applicant before you (who just came from station 5) will be giving you instructions.** To clarify, you will act once as the person giving instructions and then act once as the person receiving instructions – **both times you will be with different applicants.**

Now that we got the logistics out of the way, let's continue on what is important for this station. For this situation, the person that is giving instructions will be shown a completed version of a product (this can be a picture, multiple pictures, a completed figure with Legos, etc.) and the person that is receiving the instructions will be given the tools to create this product (blank paper and pencil, Lego pieces, etc.). The goal is to give instructions to the other team member to build/draw what you see in front of you – the completed product. Here is the caveat: your backs will be against each other. That's right. The person receiving instructions will not be able to see the completed version of the product and the person giving instructions cannot assess how the other team member is doing during this process. You may only rely on constant communication to be able to complete the task.

Teamwork Station

I will do a complete run through with an example so you may get a better idea of how you should approach this station.

Let's say you just approached the teamwork station and you read the prompt outside the door. The prompt will normally explain how the teamwork station works. The buzzer goes off and you enter the room. Greet both the evaluator and the person that you will be providing instructions to. There will be two chairs that are placed against each other; sit in one of those chairs and begin the instructional process.

- **Start by giving an introduction to the person you will be giving instructions to.** "Hey my name is Hayk, and I have a picture here of figures and I will be giving you step by step instructions so you can replicate the picture. How about after each step, you can confirm to me that you completed that step, and we can move on to the next step. How does that sound?" Notice how welcoming and professional this sounds. **Most applicants will not do this. They will sit in the chair and spew out instructions, but you are working in a team and the other member needs to feel involved.**

- **Communicate effectively** - Give step by step instructions that are detailed. Do not use the words, "here, there, or over there." What does that mean? Your team member cannot see what you see, so be as descriptive as possible. I will use the figure below as an example for giving instructions.

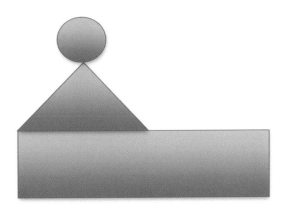

Teamwork Station

You: "Hey my name is Hayk, and I have a picture here of figures and I will be giving you step by step instructions so you can replicate the picture. How about after each step, you can confirm to me that you completed that step, and we can move on to the next step. Feel free to let me know if you have any questions before moving on. How does that sound?"

Other Individual: "Great, that sounds good to me. Let's start."

You: "Awesome. Okay what I am looking at is a composite figure of three shapes. Let's start with the first shape. I want you to draw rectangle, that is longer horizontally. To be specific, its horizontal sides are about 3 times longer than the vertical sides."

Other Individual: "Ok, got it, next."

You: "Okay next were going to draw a triangle that will be placed on top of this rectangle. The base of this triangle will start on the upper left corner of the rectangle and extend out to about halfway towards the upper right corner of the triangle. This is an equilateral triangle, so all sides of the triangle will be similar in length."

Other Individual: "Okay one second, I am about to finish drawing this. Okay, next."

You: "Perfect, now we will draw the third and last shape which is a circle. This circle is going to sit on the tip of the triangle. To get an idea of how big this circle is, make the diameter of the circle about half the size of one of the sides of the triangle."

Other Individual: "Okay great!"

Notice how descriptive my language is. I am including the size references, relative positions, and any other figurative language to carefully guide my team member through this process. Also, notice how engaged the team member is. You want them to feel important and an equal player during this time. **This is really important – probably more important than describing the figure itself.**

Teamwork Station

Realistically, you will not have enough time to finish giving instructions. There will either be too many pictures or the figure will have too many parts for you to explain each in the time you have. **Finishing the figure does not matter.** I have heard of applicants complaining that they should have had more time to finish, but they are missing a clear point. After the time runs out, the interviewer will ask you and your team member to turn around and to discuss ways to improve after revealing what your team mate drew. Meaning, what would you do differently if you and your team member had to do this task again? **This is what is important – not if you finished or not.** Your response and engagement with your team mate is what is being evaluated. **You want to be encouraging, supportive, and add one or two constructive improvements surrounded by compliments and praise on their work.** It should sound something like this:

"I think overall we did a good job as a team. My teammate did an excellent job following directions and executing the game plan. I would be more efficient and aware of time if we had to repeat this task in order to complete it with the time constraint. Granted, if we were given more time I believe we would finish the task in an appropriate fashion."

Your team mate then will then continue this tone after your lead. He/she will thank you for your instructions and the fact that you were clear, and they will probably add one improvement. Now, imagine how this looks to the interviewer. You and another stranger were given a task to complete within 5 minutes; you teamed up, gave each other an encouraging exchange of compliments, and are on the same page. **This is the heart and soul of this station. You need to be able to achieve this with your team mate.**

I firmly believe you will be evaluated on three things:

- **Your ability to communicate** – Give details in your instructions, be clear, and keep it simple.

- **Your ability to work in a team** – Include your team mate from the beginning by giving them an introduction and making them feel engaged.

- **How you give constructive criticism to improve** – Suggest improvements that are surrounded by three times as many compliments/praise to your team member.

CHAPTER 7

Role Playing Station

Role Playing Station

We have reached the notorious role playing or acting station! It can be the scariest experience in the world or the most enjoyable. This will depend on how much fun you have with it. My biggest suggestion is to pretend you are having a good time with your friends, and just act it out with confidence. The evaluator will not be expecting you to pull off Leonardo DiCaprio acting. With that said, do not be shy or timid as you enter your role-playing. Keep in mind that you are interacting with another trained actor, so might as well tango with this actor.

Before I explain the scenarios below I want to mention that the role playing station is evaluating you on the delivery of **something**. Whether it is comforting, reassuring or helping someone, **you will be evaluated on your interaction with this person.** Depending on the scenario, you may be delivering bad news or helping someone with their anxiety attack. It does not matter because the interviewer wants to see how well you can mesh with another stranger and have your presence be an impact.

For one of my acting scenarios, I literally walked into the room and put my hand on the actor's shoulder as I started talking. My body language was confident while at the same time I tried to be as attentive as possible. To be more comforting, I kneeled down to the actor's sitting position and continued talking. Notice how different this is than me sitting down across from the actor with a table in between us. **Your body language and your positioning in the room is equally as important as what you say.**

1. Imagine that you have backstage tickets to a play. The first act just finished and as you wait for the second, you notice one of the artists nervously pacing back and forth. They seem to be nervous for their act. Use this time to interact with her.

[Walk into the room]

Me: "Hello, I noticed you from back there. How are you doing?"

Actor: "Um, who are you? Um how do you think I'm feeling, I can't even remember any of my lines."

[Approach actor]

Role Playing Station

Me: "I'm one of the audience members, I just wanted to come by and say I'm rooting for you and excited to see you up there."

Actor: "Well, gee thanks... I'm just really nervous. Ugh, I knew I shouldn't have pursued this. I should've just become a lawyer like my parents told me to."

Me: "I disagree, I think the fact that you had the guts to pursue something you truly wanted shows that you have lots of courage. Not a lot of people can do that. Look, I know these moments can seem tough, but I know you will do well! Have confidence in yourself!"

[Walk closer to the actor and position yourself in front of actor]

Actor: "It's so much easier said than done. I mean you're not the one that's going to go up there right now!"

Me: "Yes, you're right. I'm not the one that's going to go up there, but you know what, I'll be in the crowd cheering you on. Me and the rest of that audience. We can't wait until you kill it up there."

Actor: "Well, thanks that was nice."

[Grab a water bottle that was sitting on the table, kneel down to actor's level and offer her some water to drink]

Me: "Here, drink some of this water, take a deep breath, and relax your mind. Everything is going to be fine."

[Pat the actor on the shoulder and comfort her]

Actor: "Thank you. That made me feel so much better."

Role Playing Station

This is a short example of a scenario that you may expect. Notice how in control and relaxed I seem in regard to acting out this station. **Even more so that I improvised and grabbed her water bottle from the table to offer her a drink.** Remember to keep your body language confident, your tone relaxed, and your language positive. When you do this, you will have the wit necessary to make clever responses and to make fast decisions that can have a huge impact (e.g., kneeling down to actor's level, improvising with a tissue box or a water bottle, putting your hand on actor's shoulder, etc.).

CHAPTER 8

Type Writing Station

Type Writing Station

The type-writing station is fairly straightforward. There will be a prompt asking you a resume type question or a traditional medical school question and you will have anywhere from 5-8 minutes to type your response. I have included the main questions that you may be asked for this station.

1. Describe your journey into medicine and the experiences that have shaped your decision to pursue the medical field.

2. Why do you think you would be a good physician?

3. What is the biggest challenge you have faced and how has that shaped the person you are right now?

These questions can be easily prepared beforehand and if you really know your application well, you may answer it on the spot. These are more secondary-type questions but are harder because of the time constraint. You only have two minutes to organize your thoughts. Considering this, do not expect to write a masterpiece – no one will be able to mention every experience or detail. **What you must do is reflect the same theme or ideas as in your primary and secondary applications.** This is important. I **firmly believe this is a tactic by medical schools to see how much of your application is really you.** For example, let's say you emphasized that you have a strong interest in academic medicine on your application. Before entering this station, you somehow end up scrambling for ideas and mention public health or other clinical activities that led you to decide medicine was a good choice for you - instead of mentioning your research and teaching experiences. This will look like a discrepancy. **Avoid this at all costs.**

CHAPTER 9

Example Scenarios

Example Scenarios

-- --

1. You are hired by the local zoo as an animal trainer to work with a new pair of chimpanzee monkeys. The zoo would like to set up an exhibit that allows the pair of chimpanzees to safely interact with the zoo visitors. This requires that the chimpanzees be fully trained and responsive to commands. Upon meeting the pair of chimpanzees, you observe that they are very occupied and distracted. Despite offering treats, you are not able to get their full attention. Please discuss your plan to succeed in training these two chimpanzees.

2. You are a nutritionist working with a family doctor in your community. Along with the family doctor, you have formulated a care plan for a patient who was recently diagnosed with diabetes (type II). The patient is unaware that they have diabetes. Upon their return to see you, they feel great and ask for the results of their recent blood sugar testing. Please discuss how you would proceed in this situation.

3. You are working as an assistant manager for a large corporation and have been with the company for 3 years. The current manager of your department was promoted to her current position two years ago and after her promotion, "the power has gone to her head." She is overly demanding and has a my way or the highway attitude. After a meeting, she approaches you and tells you that your job may be in jeopardy unless you can see things eye to eye with her. How would you respond to this situation?

4. The proverbial phrase, "tell me who your friends are and ill tell you who you are" is used to represent the idea that like attracts like. A number of medical schools automatically grant admissions' interviews to applicants whose parents are former graduates and alumni of the program. As the newly hired dean of a medical school, a meeting with the members of the admissions' committee has been called to discuss whether the practice of automatically granting legacy interviews to alumni children should continue or cease to exist. Discuss whether you feel legacy interviews for alumni children should continue or cease to exist.

Example Scenarios

5. A general observation in the pharma industry is that the consumer costs of prescription medications are significantly higher in the US compared to other developed countries. A principle to account for the differential cost of prescription medications among developed countries is that the US bears the largest burden of drug research and development and subsequently must pass this burden on to US consumers. Please discuss whether you think this principle is valid or acceptable.

6. In 2012, the American academy of family physicians published an article exploring the impact of physician role models. They used scenarios involving physicians offering smoking cessation and lifestyle counseling to their smoking patients. According to the research, patients have more confidence in preventive health counseling advice from non-smoking physicians compared to their smoking counterparts. They study also concluded that physicians with medical unhealthy personal lifestyle habits are less likely to counsel their patients about adopting a healthy lifestyle. Discuss whether physicians have a duty to act as a healthy role models for their patients.

7. You are a child support worker for child protection services and receive an anonymous call from a concerned neighbor regarding a case of suspected child abuse. She tells you that a couple and their two younger children, ages 9 and 13, have recently moved into the apartment next door to her. She has noticed several bruises on the children's faces along with poor hygiene. When she questions the children directly in front of their parents, they seem reserved and unwilling to talk and say the bruises are a result of their own carelessness. Discuss how you would respond to this call.

8. Recently, the Prime Minister of Canada raised the issue of deterrent fees (a small charge, say $10, which everyone who initiates a visit to a health professional would have to pay at the first contact) as a way to control health care costs. The assumption is that this will deter people from visiting their doctor for unnecessary reasons. Consider the broad implications of this policy for health and health care costs. For example, do you think the approach will save health care costs? At what expense? Discuss this issue with the interviewer.

Example Scenarios

9. Due to the shortage of physical therapists in rural communities, it has been suggested that physical therapy programs preferentially admit students who are willing to commit to a 2 or 3, year tenure in an under-serviced area upon graduation. Consider the broad implications of this policy for health and health care costs. For example, do you think the approach will be effective? At what expense? Discuss this issue with the interviewer.

10. A Hispanic mother brings in her son for treatment for asthma. He has been to the hospital 3 times for asthma exacerbations. As you talk to her, she states she does not want medications for her child, but would rather have "natural" remedies prescribed by her family "curandera." What are the issues here? How would you approach this mother and her child?

11. Dr. Smith recommends homeopathic medicines to his patients. There is no scientific evidence or widely accepted theory to suggest that homeopathic medicines work. He recommends homeopathic medicine to people with mild and non-specific symptoms such as fatigue, headaches and muscle aches, because he believes that it will do no harm, but will give them reassurance. Consider the ethical problems that Dr. Smith's behavior might pose. Discuss these issues with the interviewer.

12. Why do you want to be a physician? Discuss this question with the interviewer.

13. Universities are commonly faced with the complicated task of balancing the educational needs of their students and the cost required to provide learning resources to a large number of individuals. As a result of this tension, there has been much debate regarding the optimal size of classes. One side argues that smaller classes provide a more educationally effective setting for students, while others argue that it makes no difference, so larger classes should be used to minimize the number of instructors required. Discuss your opinion on this issue with the examiner.

Example Scenarios

14. The parking garage at your place of work has assigned parking spots. On leaving your spot, you are observed by the garage attendant as you back into a neighboring car, a BMW, knocking out its left front headlight and denting the left front fender. The garage attendant gives you the name and office number of the owner of the neighboring car, telling you that he is calling ahead to the car owner, Greg. The garage attendant tells you that Greg is expecting your visit. Enter Greg's office.

15. A general principal in the pharmaceutical industry is that a drug is not real unless it has been tested in English-speaking countries. A "real drug" is one that actually works and can be an economically viable product. Do you think this general principal is valid and/or acceptable? Discuss this question with the interviewer.

16. When you enter the room there will be a sheet of paper that illustrates how to complete an origami (paper folding) project. On the other side of the room there is another candidate who can't look at you, but who has a blank piece of paper. Verbally guide your colleague to completion of the origami project. You have five minutes to complete the project after which you will be given three minutes to discuss with your colleague any difficulties that arise during your communication.

17. Should the government directly fund the education of medical students as opposed to funding other professions such as law and engineering? Discuss this question with the interviewer.

18. A lot of people you work with have noticed that many random things which they own are going missing. It appears that some personal items that are not extremely valuable have gone missing over the course of the last two months. Regardless, many of your co-workers are concerned. What suggestions would you bring to an upcoming meeting with your co-workers about finding a way to address this issue?

Example Scenarios

-- --

19. While driving with your friends to a party, you are carefully paying attention to the street signs as directions are being given to you by your passenger-seat companion. Unfortunately, there is a tricky turn that your companion almost misses but mentions to you right as you are passing the intersection going at 40 miles per hour. As you try to adjust, you swerve into a car coming down in the parallel lane and cause an accident. What do you do next?

20. You are on an airplane and after you have taken off for a 4-hour flight, a baby sitting right behind your seat starts to cry. As time goes on, even while you have earphones, the screams don't stop. The parent accompanying the child keeps trying to quiet the baby down but to no avail. For every passing minute, the screams get louder and louder. What do you do?

21. You are playing the card game hearts, and your partner is demonstrably less skilled and experienced than you. After a few hands, you both are down by over 100 points as a team, mostly because your partner keeps apologizing for making stupid mistakes during the game. What do you say to your partner?

22. Many Native Americans believe they come from the land. This is important in discussing ceremonies about death. You are a funeral home manager looking after funeral arrangements for a 55-year-old who passed away two weeks ago. He has not left behind any advanced directives. His wife of 33 years strongly believes he should be buried whereas his parents strongly oppose a burial and believe he should be cremated with his ashes scattered over the land. You cannot proceed any further with the funeral arrangements until a decision is made regarding the type of burial. Discuss the course of action you would take.

Printed in Poland
by Amazon Fulfillment
Poland Sp. z o.o., Wrocław